Insignificant Me!

Insignificant Me!

Ruth Washington

authorHOUSE®

AuthorHouse™
1663 Liberty Drive
Bloomington, IN 47403
www.authorhouse.com
Phone: 1-800-839-8640

Published by AuthorHouse   09/05/2012

ISBN: 978-1-4772-6479-9 (sc)
ISBN: 978-1-4772-6477-5 (hc)
ISBN: 978-1-4772-6478-2 (e)

Library of Congress Control Number: 2012915965

INTRODUCTION

The reason this book is titled "Insignificant Me" is because as a registered voter, I really feel I am insignificant in the whole scheme of things. All the pundits, politicians, and people of importance have had their say; I only thought it appropriate to express a simple voter's perspective from one of the 99%. The candidates will do and say anything that's required to get us to vote for them. Once they are elected, they forget the voters, the primary reason they got elected. I didn't see any Lobbyist voting as a Lobbyist, or corporations; they simply received one vote per person, the same as me. So, why should there be Lobbyist or corporations involved in our political process? It makes the ruling by our supposedly Supreme Court all the more asinine. It is ludicrous to allow corporations to spend as much money as they want to buy or influence the election. The Supreme Court is not so supreme, they do make mistakes and are not infallible. We want to police every other country's political process, but who in the hell is policing ours? No one died and left us in charge of everything that goes on in the world.

Justice Antonin Scalia while on an interview with Piers Morgan supposedly said the following: "I don't think any of my colleagues on any cases vote the way they do for political reasons. They vote the way they do because they have their own judicial philosophy." I beg to differ with Justice Scalia. My impression is the Supreme Court's job is to simply interpret the law, their own judicial philosophy should never enter into a case. Maybe that is where the misunderstanding is. For you to be deciding a case based solely on your own judicial philosophy, which everyone knows is Republican is a travesty.

Each elected candidate's objective should be to represent their constituents to the very best of their ability. There is one thing I will never understand about electing someone to represent a certain district. The elected official only represents those who voted for him/her, who is supposed to represent those who didn't vote for them. Are the voters who voted for someone else, not entitled to any representation for the term of the elected official, whether it be a Democrat or Republican? I have heard elected officials use the term "mandate," but to me you can only have a mandate if you receive 100% of the votes. If you get 55% of the votes, what is supposed to happen to the other 45% or who is supposed to represent them who didn't vote for you? I do not think our forefathers meant for the minority voters to go without representation for the term of the elected official. This is my opinion only, what do I know; that is why we should compromise.

When your whole plan from jump street is to ensure the President is a one term President, how is that doing the will of the people? Your plans did not coincide with the people's plan, to work together to solve this country's problems. This is what the people voted for, but you have a different agenda and it does not include the people's wishes. How arrogant can you be? Your objective should be to represent all of your constituents, not just your party. Is this too much to ask of you? It is the same with the taxes, the majority of the people think fairness should prevail, and every survey has shown that; yet you insist on keeping things status quo. Isn't that arrogance to think you know what is better for this country than the majority of the voters?

In Robert Draper's book, it is alleged that "the GOP's Anti Obama Campaign started the night of the inauguration. The reason I am not surprised or shocked is because I wouldn't have expected any less.

Supposedly 15 Republicans and strategist were together figuring out how to sabotage the newly elected President and his ideas. He didn't stand a chance, because it was never their intention to work with him. If they truly wanted what was best for this country as they have pretended, they would have worked with him to tackle some of the ills that affect us. In spite of this he still managed to get something done. It really makes an impact to get a credit card statement that provides you with two alternatives for paying it off. The Affordable Care Act (ACA), and a student's ability to stay on parents insurance until the age of 26 was a blessing. We wanna be top dog or leader of the pack, yet in all these years no one has produced a viable healthcare plan for the uninsured.

I have a very good friend who I admire for her wisdom. We were discussing President Obama one day and she says to me "Do you know why they call it the White house; because no one but Whites were ever supposed to sit in it." It really gives you food for thought. Why didn't they call it The Capitol or something like this? Why did it have to be the White House?

If Rush Limbaugh can get away with some of his absurd hallucinations, why can't I have any?

INSIGNIFICIENT Me!

Because of a family health disorder, I find it easier to articulate my thoughts on paper by writing them down. Well, it is the year and the time I dread the most. It is the Presidential election year, where we elect or appoint a President for the next four years. It is a time we are forced to endure as we listen to all the lies, promises, innuendo, etc. Why can't the politicians we have campaigning for office simply tell us what their plans are for making our lives easier? I'll tell you why, because they simply don't have a plan. Don't waste my time telling me what Joe Blow has not done for me. Simply state your plans if you have any, allow me to make the decision of who I think will do the best job for the country or who is the lesser of two evils. As a cousin of mine used to say often times "playing upon my little intelligence."

I liked the fact that all the Republican debates were not on every network. Don't automatically assume everyone wants to hear all this rhetoric on every network. Each network should take turns donating time to the candidates and debates? In this way those who are interested can tune in and those not interested can do something else.

One of my pet peeves concerns the amount of money spent to make the public believe all the lies, promises, innuendo and rhetoric told to us. What is even more disturbing is how gullible some of us are. Why isn't that money spent to pay down the deficit? If the politicians are truly concerned about the deficit, isn't this a viable start on reducing the deficit?

It was alleged Meg Whitman spent over $141.5 million dollars of her own money in a losing campaign for Governor of California. Think of all the good she could have done with all that money if she had donated it to some school district or some other entity in the State experiencing financial problems. She would have gotten more votes this way, than the other. She would have gotten my vote, because I would have said to myself "she really does care and will help the State." Rarely do I vote Republican; I will if they have the right message. Instead, she may as well have wiped her ass with $141.5 million dollars and flushed it down the toilet for the good it did.

What is it going to take for us to get serious and do something about our deficit? My mama always said "charity begins at home, and then spreads abroad." When other nations request our assistance, why can't we just say no, I don't understand. We are not in a position to help ourselves, how can we help anybody else? Our own people are in dire straits. Allow us time to step back, regroup and get ourselves together; then we may be able to help others. It would be foolish of me to loan you money to pay your bills and I don't have enough money to pay my own bills.

INSIGNIFICANT ME

This book is dedicated to our daughter and son. It is a minute synopsis of my childhood as I remember. I was born in a small town of Ferriday, LA. when Jim Crow (segregation) was the rule of the day. My dad had a fourth grade education and my mom was considered illiterate. She couldn't read or write. My mom didn't know her name in box car letters. What she lacked in education, she more than made up the difference in mother wit. Mother wit was/is the usage of common sense, which so many of us today do not possess.

I was the baby in a family of eight children. I don't know if there was such a thing as welfare at that time or not, but we certainly could have used some help. We were so poor, we spelled poor with one o (por); we couldn't afford two o's. At that time diversity was a none issue. We had two Chinese families in town. One I was very familiar with; I thought their last name was Chinaman. How would I know their last name was Lee, which I found out after I was an adult? My mother used to always say "go out to John Chinaman and get me thus and so," so I thought their last name was Chinaman. I want to apologize to the family now, what a racist I was and didn't even know it. The same is true for the other family in town who was not Black or White, they were Mexican. They were referred to as Joe the Mexican who operated a fruit stand; I am embarrassed at my ignorance. I want to apologize to that family also. Even though we were poor, I never knew we were poor growing up as a child.

Mother had a first cousin who lived across the street from us named Truelove Jordan. I can recall instances when mother sent me across the street to borrow money. There were times when she borrowed a quarter, or one or two dollars. Funny, I never recall paying the money back, but never did cousin Truelove say to me "Tell her I don't have it." Cousin Truelove wore thick glasses and kept her money in a coin purse in the chifferobe. A chifferobe at that time functioned as a closet where you kept clothes and it had a small area for you to store important documents or papers. She would immediately get her coin purse and give me whatever amount mother had requested. If it was a quarter, it was usually for me to attend some function they were having at school.

From my parents I learned what the face of love looked like, even though I cannot recall one time they ever said "I love you," you knew from their actions they loved you. They exhibited this love with their brothers, sisters, children and all the rest of the family. The brothers and sisters who lived in town called or visited each other daily.

My dad had a sister named Janie, whose mind was not too good. The talk was someone had voodooed her for her husband and she was never right after that. However, she always remembered my father's birthday. I will never forget the time she baked him a cake. She said "Brother Cliff I baked you a cake for your birthday, I didn't have any baking powder, so I put a little starch in it." I was lying in bed the other morning and I couldn't help shed some tears at the thought of her, the epitome of her love was so overwhelming. I also had a sister named Eliza (pig) for short. Eliza was a phenomenal cook; she could cook a pot of beans and leave them on the stove cooking while she went to town. When she got back, they would be perfect. She baked a mean pineapple, pecan and coconut cake. My daughter calls it "the heart attack cake." My sister had six (6) children and every time she got pregnant Aunt Janie would give her a can of peaches. I don't know what they were supposed to symbolize, but that was a lot of peaches. Who knows in her little mind what they were supposed to mean, but that was her way of showing love to those who meant so much to her.

My dad also had a sister named Julia Jordan, who owned 18 1/2 acres of land in the country. Every Sunday she would bring fresh churned buttermilk to us and we would have cornbread and milk. We would have the cornbread hot and waiting for her arrival. If she was late, I was disappointed. My first memory of this ritual was my aunt driving a horse and wagon. Later on she started to bring the milk in a truck.

When my oldest brother Leroy got married, he and his wife Martha lived with us for a short time until they bought their own place. Mother taught Martha everything. When she married Leroy she couldn't boil water. I can remember at Christmas time all the women came to our house and mother taught them how to bake cakes. Mother had a large stainless steel dishpan she made her cakes in. She had to cream the butter and sugar with her hands, because at that time we didn't know what a mixer was. I don't know if they were available or not, I know we didn't have one. Mother would make up enough batter for 3 to 4 cakes at a time. She always made the first layer of the cake a "try." She could taste the "try" and tell you exactly what the cake needed, and she would add the missing ingredient. I don't have to tell you my sister Eliza got her cooking skills from our mother.

I was born in the year 1943 in the small town of Ferriday, LA. And when I say racist that is exactly what I mean. I can remember picking cotton at an early age, although I don't recall my exact age. I was so excited the first day I went to pick cotton. Now that I think about it, it was a dehumanizing experience. A truck came around town with a covering on top of it, and all the cotton pickers sat on makeshift benches in the truck with head rags and old clothes on, looking awful. Just think, if this truck was involved in an accident, all of us would've probably been killed.

The very first time I picked cotton, I picked 50 lbs. You were paid by the lbs. you picked. At that time it might have been $3.00 for 100 lbs. After my initial pick of 50 lbs. I never picked more than 35 lbs. after that. After about a month of this picking only 35 lbs., my mother said to me "Ruth you don't make enough to pay for your lunch, it's no use in you going anymore." Boy that was music to my ears, so I never picked any cotton after that. You see the main reason I couldn't pick any cotton, was because I was a scary cat. If I saw one of those big black hairy worms lying on my sack, I was not going to do anything but look for them the rest of the day. I called them black hairy worms; now I know they were caterpillars.

When I went to school, Mrs. Green flunked me in the first grade. I didn't understand at the time. It was probably the best thing she could have done for me, because beginning about the fourth grade I was strictly an A, B student. I can remember in grades 4 thru 8, I made the honor roll each grading period with A's and B's. We always had an assembly in the gym and the Principal, Mr. Clark would announce the Honor Roll winners. He would call my name with having 9 A's or 7 A's and 2 B's.

Our Principal was a phenomenal Principal. If you came late to school, he would be standing outside waving his hands and say "Go back! Go back!" and you did. I also remember there was a table full of us and he came into the library where we were talking. At that time study hall was held in the school library. He motioned for us to come with him and we did. He put the whole table of us on yard duty, which was his favorite punishment for any student caught doing something wrong.

First, I need to digress for a moment. When I went to school we were totally segregated. We had classes in a building on the main street and when I was in 4th grade I remember we had classes in the old Masonic hall building. When I was in the building on Front Street, I can remember students would be assigned to pick up the pots of food for lunch and serve them. They had to go to the kitchen and pick up the pots. The kitchen was located in a totally separate building from the classroom. I would not trade my experience I had with school for anything, because we had teachers who really and truly cared whether you learned or not. My Home Economics teacher Grace Hayes told me one time "even though you deserve a better grade, I'm going to give you this D, because I know you can do better."

I remember one Thanksgiving my group was assigned the task of cooking the hen. Miss. Hayes was a stickler for following the recipe. I told her we should parboil the hen first, then bake it. She said "Ruth you just follow the recipe." We did and that hen was so tough each student had to take their piece home and finish cooking it. She said to me afterwards, "Ruth maybe we should have parboiled it first." I said "Miss Hayes my momma has cooked too many of those hens for me not to know what to do." At that time and still now, if you purchase a hen in the south, it requires a long time to cook and that's what I love about them. The only time I bought a hen in California, I was thoroughly disappointed, because it cooked too fast and did not have the same flavor. To this day when I go south, I want to have a hen.

I thank God I had the teachers I had in school. Some of the more memorable ones were Mrs. Jenkins, Mrs. Buford, Miss. Shepherd, Mrs. Woods, Mrs. Porter, Mrs. Alexander, Miss Edwards, Mr. Hayes, Mrs. Brooks and Principals Mr. A. D. Clark and Mrs. Washington. These were phenomenal teachers in my life, and I will be forever grateful to them.

My mother worked all her life as a maid. She worked for some good White folks and some not so good. She started out making $10 a week for six days and graduated to $15 a week. She worked for the Dinger family and the Crum family. They were really good to my mom. Mrs. Dinger had a daughter named Gloria and she wore beautiful clothes. All of her hand me downs were given to my mom. When my mom passed in 1986, Mr. Crum bought half a tub full of fish for our family.

The last family I remember my mother worked for was the Henderson family. They were one of the poorest families I could remember and they had no class. The father would sit at the table and fart and say "Beans, beans eat them hot, the more you eat the more you fart." The mother owned a beauty shop attached to her house, and wore white uniforms. Every Thursday mother would bring home 4 or 5 of those uniforms for me to iron and have ready for her to carry back to work on Friday. All this she did while drawing a salary of $15 a week. There was never any social security taken out, nor was there taxes paid. I am willing to bet you this is still occurring, not only in the south, but all over. The wages might have increased, but the treatment is the same. So, if you have never walked a mile in my shoes, don't tell me to get over it. I have forgiven, but I will never forget.

There were three prominent White families in town I knew of; one was Mr. Lee Calhoun who owned a lot of property in town. Mr. Joe Pasternack owned a furniture store, and Dr. Vogt owned a drugstore. My parents bought our house from Mr. Lee Calhoun, who to me was nothing but a crook. Like I said, my mother could not read or write. How many times did we pack that black embroidered bag of her's filled with receipts up to Mr. Calhoun trying to get him to tell her how much she owed on the house. My mother kept impeccable records/receipts. We lived on 6th Street in the Black part of town and Mr. Calhoun lived straight up the same street in the White part of town. I couldn't begin to tell you how many times we did this ritual. I don't know if he ever told mother how much she owed him, but I guess he finally did because the house ended up in my dad's name.

The scene from the help about the bathroom reminded me so much of the past. My sister who died in 2009 and I used to talk about those days. She said she remembered cleaning the bathroom where she worked and flushing the toilet after cleaning. The lady of the house said to her "I don't mind if you use the toilet, just be sure to wipe the seat after you finish." My sister said she never went back to work for her again.

My sister also told me a friend of her's worked for this family. She went to work this particular day and was so hungry. The family had a biscuit left over from breakfast and she asked if she could have it. The lady said to her "No! We're going to have that for supper." Can you imagine having a leftover biscuit for supper?

Often times I look back with regret with some of the things we lost. I can remember when Black folks had everything going for them except equal opportunity and justice. On Front Street was the main drag. We had James Watkins grocery store and cleaners; at that time we called them pressing shops. We also had another Black cleaner in the next block along with a theatre where we had concerts. I can recall going to this theatre one time only, and this was the time Sam Cooke and the Soul Stirrers were playing there. This was before he got famous; he was singing Gospel at that time.

I also remember we had Rev. Skinner's store on 5th St., Mr. Roosevelt's store on 6th St., Mr. Walker's store on 7th St. and Mr. Green past 7th St. We patronized all these merchants and their establishments. Mr. Dave Reed had the one taxicab I can remember in town. Now they have none of these things I know of.

Also in the previous block on the main drag was 4th St. We had Haney's Big House, where the entire famous up and coming artist played on the Chitlin Circuit. They had a sign hanging that said "We may doze, but we never close" and they never did, because at that time clubs could stay open all night. The song "A Hole in the wall" by Mel Waiters, reminded me of those juke joints; as they were commonly called. Everybody partied and had a good time without any violence. If someone stepped on your foot, they said "excuse me" and didn't pull out a Glock and shoot you as what might happen today.

There was a time when music was music and you understood what was being said by the artist. There were artist such as Mel Waiters ("A Hole in the Wall"), he talked about going to this dive at 3 a.m. in the morning and staying until 7 a.m. having such a good time, and being in a smoke filled room with the smell of whiskey and chicken wings. Of course Mel came along much later than the earlier artists.

There was B. B. King, Bobby (Blue) Bland, *"Fever"* (Lil Willie John), *"I Stand Accused"* (Jerry Butler), *"Cry To Me"*

(Solomon Burke), *"There It Is," "I Wish It Was Me," "Give It Up And Turn It Loose," "I had It All The Time," "Can I Change My Mind,"* etc. (Tyron Davis), *"Cheaper To Keep Her," "Who's Making Love"* (Johnnie Taylor), *"Since I Met You Baby"* (Ivory Joe Hunter), *"Having A Party,"* Frankie & Johnny, *"A Change Is Gonna Come* "(Sam Cooke), *"Chokin Kind"* (Joe Simon), *"I Found A Love"* (The Falcons) and a whole plethora of artist. At one time when you went to a club you ordered a set-up, which included ice, a coke or seven-up and lemon. You purchased whatever kind of liquor you wanted that went along with your set-up.

This list also included Jazz greats such as Les McCann *"Compared To What,"* and Eddie Harris *"Listen Here,"* Jimmy Smith, Jimmy McGriff, Ramsey Lewis and others. I remember when Sam Cooke was singing R & B, he had this record *"We're Having A Party."* It included a line about *"The Cokes Are In The Icebox,"* and he didn't mean cocaine. I played Sam Cooke so much until my son loves him, especially *"A Change Is Gonna Come."*

I can also remember one time Aretha Franklin came to town when she was a young girl, the same as I was. She came to town to perform with her father, the late Rev. C. L. Franklin.

I lived in California, but I had gone home for Christmas one year. This was the year they arrested my brother for nothing. I was at my mom's house when my sister came down and told us they had arrested him and she was going to see about him. Knowing my sister and her big mouth, I decided to go with her. You had to be careful of the way you talked to White folks. When we got uptown to the jail, a deputy asked us "What y'all want?" My sister replied "We wanna see Leroy." The Deputy replied, "Well y'all can't see him tonight." He told us the main Deputy was not there, but was expected back shortly and we could wait across the street for him. Finally he came and asked us the same question, "What y'all want?" Again, my sister reiterated "We wanna see Leroy." To this request he replied, "Y'all can't see him tonight." My sister replied "Why not." The Deputy then said "Because I said so!" He then began to reach inside the car to get the keys. About this time my sister and her boyfriend showed up and wanted to know what was going on.

At that time the Deputy backed up, but who knows what would have happened if they had not shown up just at that moment. There we were, two Black women in a highly segregated town at the Police Station; they could've said anything happened. We would've been dead, and dead men/women tell no tales. Every since that encounter, I have had and still have a fear of the police. Since then I have gotten progressively better; thanks to the Police Chief in California.

I have been watching the cold case file about Frank Morris. The deputies for the town at that time had a notorious reputation. A Black person's life wasn't worth a plugged nickel. Most of the deputies were known members of the Ku Klux Klan; this was just a fact of life. One deputy DeLaughter, was so vicious and feared until he was known as "Big Frank DeLaw." I hope he is rotting in hell now for all the atrocities he committed against mankind. Frank had a shoe repair shop. In 1964 they literally burned him alive in his own repair shop. I use the term burned alive, because he didn't survive the fire he was burned too bad.

Another Black man who has been missing since 1964 was Joseph Edwards. There was talk he was skinned alive according to the underground pipeline. Can you imagine being skinned alive? I do not doubt this, because Whites in the South at that time were very vicious and committed unspeakable crimes against Blacks. Even today some are still as violent and vicious as ever.

One time I hid one of my shoes. When I was growing up, you only had one pair of shoes at a time; and you wore them until they wore out. Well, I had a pair of black and white oxfords which you couldn't wear out. I was so sick of those shoes until I hid one so my mother couldn't find it and had to buy me another pair of shoes.

One of my uncles lived in Monroe, LA. and was quite successful. I think he owned some type of flooring company. When my first cousin got married in Monroe, my uncle and his wife had a dinner party for his nephew, who was his sister's son. I will never forget as long as I live, they had barbecued chicken as a main dish. It was very good. The groom's brother and I were the same age, and sat next to each other at the dinner table. None of the family was used to eating at my uncle's house, so he whispered to me "Are you gonna get another piece of chicken?" I said 'I don't know, are you?' He replied to me "I want to get another piece." Do you know neither one of us got another piece of chicken because we were too afraid.

This is the same uncle we went to visit when we went home on vacation. My brother, my first cousin Roosevelt and I went to visit them. While they were showing us around their beautiful home, my aunt pulled me to the side and asked "Baby do you want a sandwich, I ain't got but one?" Since I was the only woman in the group, I surmised that was the reason she chose me. I told her no. When I told my brother and cousin what happened, my brother was really hurt because he loved his family. Immediately after we left there my cousin took us to a seafood place and we had dinner.

I had the honor and privilege of celebrating my aunt's 104th birthday with her. I invited her and four of her nieces to have lunch with us. We sat around the dining table, ate and talked for about 4 hours. I had the occasion to talk to one of my first cousins I rarely see, and that was a treat. I told her about the problem I was having trying to access my maternal grandmother's roots. My grandmother was supposedly born in Mississippi, only I don't know where in Mississippi. She proceeded to tell me about one of the things her mother told her. One was a lot of Blacks were blindfolded and crossed over from Mississippi to Louisiana. I had never been told or ever heard of this.

I recall talking and visiting with another first cousin before she passed, and we had a very interesting conversation. She was sharing with me some of the atrocities they were forced to live under. She showed me a pass Blacks had to have in their possession in order to go from one place to another. She also had a bill of sale for a car showing the purchase price of $300. I regret not asking her for a copy of these two documents to keep.

When our kids were small, we used to exchange kids from my car to my husband's car in the parking lot where he worked. We couldn't afford a babysitter and wanted to spend as much time as possible with them. I have always been blessed enough to work within 15 to 20 minutes from home; that way I could always run home if I needed to. My husband got off at 4 p.m. and I had to be at work at 4 p.m. I got to his job at 3:45 p.m., left the kids in the car in the parking lot, and he came out at 4 p.m. and they all went home. I had already cooked dinner and left it for them. We were blessed because people at that time were a lot more trustworthy. There is no way you could do that today.

We had two beautiful children who didn't give us many problems, and we are grateful. We also didn't let them get away with anything. We had a dent in the hallway wall for about a year. Our son got smart with his father and he put him against the wall. He always remembered that. One time after, I had gone to work and left my daughter who was then 12 or 13 years old and son at home. She was supposed to be watching him and I was teaching her how to cook also at that time. I called home and asked to speak to her. My son said, "She sleep momma." I called again a few minutes later. Again he said, "She sleep momma". I made one additional call and he repeated the same thing "She sleep momma." I said "Wake her up." He replied "I can't she's not here." I immediately left work, jumped in my car and came home (15 mins.). She had gone around the corner to her friend's apartment to visit. When she finally returned, I was waiting for her. I tore her ass up with an extension cord for leaving my baby alone in the house with beans cooking on the stove. She was 4 years older than him. We never had a problem after that, she never forgot. This tells you, if there are consequences for your actions, next time you will think if I do this what will happen to me. In this day and age, that would be called child abuse; but I will tell you this, they were better kids with more discipline than today's kids with less discipline. We had better kids and never needed a nanny to teach us how to discipline or raise our kids.

I can remember an instance when I was in the kitchen cooking and my daughter was sitting on a stool. She had to be 3 or 4 years old. I was trying to teach her she was Black. So, I said to my daughter "If anybody ask you what race or nationality you are; you are to tell them you're Black." She shook her head and said to me "Oh no momma, I'm not Black." I repeated this to her two more times the same identical way. The third time I raised my voice because I'm really getting irritated now so I said, "Now look! If anybody ask you what race or nationality you are, tell them you're Black." Again she responded "Oh no momma, I'm not Black. I'm brown. Uncle James is Black." James was her Godfather, but she always referred to him as Uncle James. She was so right on. I suppose she said to herself, if Uncle James is Black and I am brown, how can both of us be classified as Black. So even at that age children can tell the difference between the colors. Uncle James was my first cousin and her Godfather.

When my daughter was in elementary school, she went to one of the best schools in our city. Most of the children she went to school with lived in the school area and she was bussed in. She came home one day and asked "What kind of jeans do I have on?" I said to her "What do you mean?." She responded "Are they Gloria Vanderbilt's or who?" I said "They are K-Mart, J C Penny or the cheapest I could find. If you want somebody's name across your ass, you'd better have someone put your name back there." She had never asked me since that day about designer wear and the only time she will buy anything designer is if it's on sale, she really likes it and it's a good deal.

One time I cut my foot really bad. All my mom did was make sure there was no glass left in it, cleaned it real good and put a piece of salt pork on the cut and tied a rag round it. We played outside in the summer a lot of times without any shoes on. The pavement was so hot I don't understand how we could not have shoes on. Of course we played in the yard, which was mostly dirt. You see, at that time there was no such thing as going to the doctor. The main reason being the expense, and the other reason there were no Black doctors in town I knew of. During those years, children played outside from sun up till sun down. I cannot recall one instance of ever going to the doctor.

My father had a first wife with whom he had a son. I can remember him having one leg shorter than the other; a result of falling off the porch when he was young and never seeing or being treated by a doctor. He lived in New Orleans.

Try as hard as I might, I cannot remember having a fat school mate. We might have had a few teachers who were considered overweight. I consider them voluptuous. The reason is a combination of things. You always had home cooked meals prepared for you, there were no fast food places, and you ate what was put in front of you on your plate. Most of the juke joints sold food, but who could afford to buy? Even the food they sold was better than most fast food nowadays. They sold dishes such as gumbo, pork chops and fried chicken. The fried chicken was served with french fries, a piece of lettuce with a slice of tomato on top of it with a glob of mayonnaise on top of that. This served as your vegetable (salad). They had terrific cooks who were all Black. I cannot recall one instance of ever having a green salad such as we fix today. A green salad at that time consisted of lettuce, tomato and mayonnaise; I don't recall having salad dressing. As a matter of fact, I had a brother-in-law who ate nothing green, and he lived to be three days shy of his 82nd birthday. All he ever ate were fried foods. He didn't like anything else.

Children were not allowed to listen to grown-up conversations at that time, unless you eavesdropped. I can recall one time my mother was telling us this practice, and told the story of what happened to them one time for listening in on grown up conversations.

They were listening under the porch and her parents mentioned Sally had broken her leg (pregnant). So they're sitting on the porch on Sunday and Sally comes walking down the street. They yelled out "We thought you broke your leg." My mom says they got the worst ass whipping later on for that comment.

I can remember my Aunt Ellen coming over to visit, and I heard her say "James (her son) and Maxine are having a baby. It may not be his, but it was caught in his net." I didn't have the faintest idea what she meant, but after I grew up and moved to California, I knew instantly what she meant because the child turned out not to be his but another gentleman's I knew.

It is too bad, we learned better; but we now have worse children. You wanna talk about child abuse, they did it in those times but we were better children. How many children did you have killing their parents or other children? I can recall being in 6th grade, Mr. Everett Washington was my teacher. At that time teachers were allowed to spank your kids in school for misbehaving. Mr. Washington beat one of my classmates so bad until his mother came to school to find out why. I don't know or can't remember what my classmate had done, but I do remember the beating. Our parents preached, "I brought you into this world and I will take you out," and we believed this. They had no fear of you or anyone else. We thought they meant every word they said. I am truly grateful and thankful for the parents I had and for my upbringing.

I have been told my paternal grandfather was killed at a young age. He was hitchhiking a ride on the train after shopping, fell off and was run over by the train. He later died because gangrene had set in. This left my grandmother with a total of 11 children; five boys and six girls and no husband. She was fortunate enough to meet and marry a man and he had 8 children. They lived in two houses side by side to accommodate this new and extended family.

I recall an instance when I was a junior in high school, two of my good friends each had a sister who died tragically in a car accident. The girls were both seniors in high school and were to graduate in 1961, the year before us. It was around Junior/Senior prom time, when they were invited to the prom in a nearby community of Jonesville, LA. From my understanding, they were hit by a driver in a big rig who had fallen asleep behind the wheel. Because of the times we were living in with Blacks having no rights or justice, neither family I know of was ever compensated nor was anybody punished for their tragic loss.

I can also recall a time when one of my friends became pregnant. My mother told me about the rumor of her being pregnant at a young age. This was the same young lady who introduced me to my future husband. My mom said to me, "I knew when she was here the other day and spit off the top step, she was pregnant. Her spit was full of foam and just as thick as it could be." I said to myself, "How the hell would she know." It's amazing the things those old folks did know. They would say things to you and you wouldn't have the faintest idea what they were talking about, once you become a young woman, it becomes clear as day. For example "it's a heap see, but a few know," meaning a lot of people see things happening, but only a few know what's actually going on.

I recall when we used to travel across country by car a lot. The first question my brother always asked was, "Do you have a bathroom?" If the answer was no, he left that station in search of one with a bathroom and would allow Blacks to use it, only then did he purchase gas for the car.

MY
Y
O
P
I
N
I
O
N
S

Opinions are just like assholes, everybody has one and these are some of mine.

AFGHANISTAN

We need to get the hell out of Afghanistan as fast as we can. How many more soldiers have to lose their lives or limbs before we exit a world where we aren't even wanted? Do we realize the toll this war has taken on our service men and women? What is the actual cost of this war? Have we factored in service people suffering from PTSD, loss of equipment, having to take care of the wounded or dead, and their families for the rest of their lives? We can't afford this war and the loss of lives of our young people. Just look at the various atrocities committed by our own soldiers. They simply do not make us popular.

HORNY SECRET SERVICE AGENTS IN COLOMBIA

I say they should all be fired; everyone who went on that advance scouting mission for the President's arrival. This is truly a job where everyone is responsible for each other and should be encouraged to snitch. If one sees another of their fellow employees doing something outside the normal realm or is unsafe, it is their responsibility to report it. We are talking about compromising the safety of the President of the United States. Let the fired employees look from the rear of the unemployment line and see what it is like to be unemployed.

With all the scandals involving the Secret Service and the GS, isn't it a little silly to try and blame the President. What role did he play in this scenario? You have different levels of authority being paid to do certain jobs and they're not fulfilling their responsibility. Sure there were supposedly Supervisors involved, but whoever is at the next level should have known what was going on and if they didn't, they were not doing their duty. It is like I said. I think in all civil service jobs employees are not doing what they are supposed to be doing, including the supervisors. If they can't or won't they should be fired. I could supervise my own mother. She would have to shit or get off the pot. I would have no problem telling her to do her job or there would be consequences. Do you honestly think those working 10 hours days, 4 days a week are actually doing that? I will guarantee you this is not happening.

What I fail to understand is what makes you think your job is guaranteed. Can't you see and hear about the high rate of unemployment? You seem oblivious to what is going on in the country about the economy and jobs. Go to the unemployment office and offer to trade places with someone in the unemployment line. I bet they would jump at the chance and do an amazing job.

If I happened to be the wife of one of those fired, they would be divorced also at the same time. There is no way in hell you would come back to me after having relations with a prostitute. What kind of diseases, etc.

did she pass on to you? Added to the fact is that you now have no job, having lost it also in the process.

APOLOGIES

I suppose an apology is supposed to make up for anything anyone has ever said or done to a person; well not in my book. People say and do things all the time. They apologize, is it heartfelt or sincere? Hell no! They are just mouthing the words to keep their jobs or keep them from appearing like fools.

Mike O'Neal apologizes for calling Michelle Obama "Mrs. YoMama." Was the apology sincere? I'll bet you $5 to a bucket of shit it was not a sincere apology. When someone has put their proverbial foot in their mouth, I'd rather they just leave it there so everyone can see what an idiot looks like. He said (supposedly) he was sorry for those he offended. Well he offended me and I don't accept his insincere apology. I am sure he really gives a shit and I don't either. I can't understand for the life of me why there is such hatred of the First Lady. Those who criticize her just cannot and will not allow themselves to believe she could be an intelligent, knowledgeable, smart, articulate, etc., Black woman. It is just too much for them to comprehend and believe that there exist strong independent Black women who know what they want, and are not afraid or ashamed to express their beliefs.

Mike O'Neal also was suppose to have sent an email involving a bible verse (Psalm 109:8) to suggest President Obama's days be few in number. I would expect the Speaker of the State House to read and understand what he reads better than a child who attended totally segregated schools in the 50's and 60's; but apparently he doesn't. The Bible is a really fascinating entity. You can't select one verse and make any meaning out of it you want it to mean. According to my Catholic Bible, Psalms Chapter 109 is a prayer of a person falsely accused, to me this should be a prayer President Obama should be praying. In the event you aren't familiar with it, it is included for your perusal.

Psalms Chapter 109
Prayer of a Person Falsely Accused

1)   O God, whom I praise, do not be silent,

2)   for wicked and treacherous mouths attack me. They speak against me with lying tongues;

3)   with hateful words they surround me, Attacking me without cause.

4)   In return for my love they slander me Even though I prayed for them.

5)   They repay me evil for good,

     Hatred for my love

     My enemies say of me:

6)   Find a lying witness,

     An accuser to stand by his right hand,

7)   That he may be judged and found guilty,

     That his plea may be in vain

8)   May his days be few;

     May another take his office.

9)   May his children be fatherless, His wife, a widow.

10) May his children be vagrant beggars, Driven from their hovels.

11) May the usurer snare all his own, Strangers plunder all he earns.

12) May no one treat him kindly or pity his fatherless children,

13) May his posterity be destroyed, His name cease in the next generation.

14) May the Lord remember his father's guilt; His mother's sin not be canceled.

15) May their guilt be always before the Lord, Till their memory is banished from the earth,

16) For he did not remember to show kindness, but hounded the wretched poor and brought death to the brokenhearted.

17) He loved cursing; may it come upon him; he hated blessing, may none come to him.

18) May cursing clothe him like a robe; may it enter his belly like water; seep into his body like oil.

19) May it be near as the clothes he wears, as the belt always around him.

20) May the Lord bring all this upon my accusers; upon those who speak evil against me.

21) But you, Lord, my God deal kindly with me for your name's sake; in your great mercy rescue me.

22) For I am sorely in need; my heart is pierced within me.

23) Like a lengthening shadow I near my end, all but swept away like the locust.

24) My knees totter from fasting; my flesh has wasted away.

25) I have become a mockery to them; when they see me, they shake their heads.

26) Help me, Lord, my God; save me in your kindness.

27) Make them know this is your hand, that you, Lord, have acted.

28) Though they curse, may you bless; shame my foes, that your servant may rejoice.

29) Clothe my accusers with disgrace; make them wear shame like a mantle.

30) I will give fervent thanks to the Lord; before all I will praise my God.

31) For God stands at the right hand of the poor to defend them against unjust accusers.

Rep. Jim Sensenbrenner apologized for saying Michelle Obama has a "large posterior" and "big butt." Okay, I want to apologize in advance for saying Jim Sensenbrenner's face to me looks like Michelle Obama's posterior. Michelle Obama is a beautifully endowed Black woman. She may not be his cup of tea, as I am sure if he has a wife or woman she is not President Obama's cup of tea. It's a funny thing a big butt is fine on Kim Kardashian, or Jennifer Lopez but not good on Michelle?

Andre Adler apologized for suggesting that assassinating President Obama is an option that should be considered by the Israeli government. Really, Mr. Adler? Have you ever before now advocated a President's assassination?

CREDIT REPORTING AGENCIES

I really have a bone to pick with the credit reporting agencies like Equifax, Experian and TransUnion; I am thoroughly disillusioned with them. In the first place, you need a Master's Degree to decipher your credit report. I always find it to be confusing. The part I didn't understand was we were currently paying more on the old loan and with the new loan our monthly payments would have been reduced considerably. How can you be qualified for the higher loan, but not qualified for a lower payment, like my mother said "mother wit" (common sense). They have the ability and power to destroy your life, but do they care what impact their decision has on your life. Hell no! They don't seem to care about destroying you at all. In the first place, they appear to be biased in favor of the creditor or bank. They list all the negative information they have accumulated on you over the years, but none of the positive. I have some questions I'd like to have answered. They are:

1. Who gave them permission to create a file on me in the first place?

2. Who gave them permission to give out my personal information to others without my authorization or consent?

3. Who are they to determine your ability to pay?

4. Why are none of the client's positive attributes never mentioned, i.e.:

   a. Customer never late

   b. Customer never missed a payment

   c. Customer always pay above minimum amount due, etc.

Exactly what is their primary responsibility when issuing a credit report on an individual? It should be to simply state the facts and not make assumptions about an individual's ability to pay. That decision should be left to the creditor. Who made you judge and jury? Only the accounts still open should be listed on the report. This would make the report easier to read and understand. A bankruptcy only stays on your report for 7 or 10 years, so why does a closed or paid off account stay on your record for 10 years? Again, mother wit, the inmates are running the asylum.

Also, things are put in a customer's credit report without verification or notification to the customer. Then a customer has to go through hell and high water to get it corrected, if they ever do. I had an occasion where someone went online and changed my billing preferences on Entergy without my consent, yet when I would call on the telephone I would have to prove who I was. Entergy allowed this person to change the information without any verification. They simply had acquired the account number. Could I go to the bank and withdraw all of someone else's money with simply the account number, which is on the bottom of every check? Because I keep immaculate records and correspondence, they had to take this off my credit report. If I had not kept records, they would have kept it on the report, otherwise I would have had no way of proving my position. It was not a matter of how much, it was simply the principle of the matter.

DRUGS

The war on Drugs is a sad affair for supposedly the way we have been waging war on them. Did you ever see young men or women in the ghetto selling drugs that had a plane, train, car or various other modes of transportation? I have always had my doubts about drugs infesting the Black community. I firmly believe drugs were brought into the Black and poor communities to destroy our people. It has always concerned me how they can have a huge drug bust and only capture the small time dealers and users.

Why don't the people who bring the drugs into the community to be sold ever get caught? Most of the people arrested in my home town where I was born barely have a car, and I don't believe most drugs are manufactured locally. So, how do they get them to sell? If they have had the suspects under surveillance for a year, shouldn't they know who they are meeting and why they are meeting with them? My theory is they stage these supposedly big drug bust to make the community think they are doing something about the drugs in the community, but to me it's all for show. When they catch some of the big time dealers and pushers, then I will believe something is being done to benefit the community.

Why don't they ever bust those in the other communities for all the cocaine they are buying and selling? There is no way I am going to believe you ever arrest the big time drug pushers, the ones making the money or drugs are only sold in the Black community. It gives you something to think about, doesn't it? I get irritated with our kids because they fell right into the drug trap that was set for them.

Recently they had a big drug bust in my home town where I was born, but did they capture the people who are really making a profit off drugs? Sure they caught a lot of the small fish, but if they put them in jail, how do you explain having subsequent drug bust all over again?

There is no way I am going to simply believe the line of bullshit I've been fed.

ENTITLEMENTS

First of all, if all the fraud, waste, etc. is cleaned up in all the government programs, we would save a fortune. It is not necessarily only the programs benefitting the poor that has a lot of waste, there is waste in all government programs. Are we sure the people we have working are giving 7 hours of work each day for 8 hours of pay? In all federal, state and county jobs there is a lot of waste. I am willing to bet you $5 to a bucket of shit there is a lot of waste. Are the workers who are supposedly doing 10 hour days, four days a week, actually doing 10 hours? I used to work for United Airlines and I guarantee you the workers weren't doing any more in 10 hours than they did in 8 hours. First of all, you have to have Supervisors who aren't afraid to do the job they are paid to do, and you have to ensure they are actually doing their jobs. This does not require breathing down the employees' neck, following them around or micromanaging. It takes a certain kind of person to be Supervisorial material and a good Manager knows one when he or she sees one.

If you really want to talk about waste, think of all the money and time wasted on Roger Clemens and Barry Bonds. Was it worth it? They were trying to prove they lied to the government, our Congress and other political figures lie all the time. I don't see them up for trial.

GENERAL SERVICES ADMINISTRATION

The GSA having a lavish bash at the taxpayers' expense shows their lack of judgment on their part. The way they were carrying on leads me to believe this was a common occurrence and they feared no consequences. Everyone involved should have been fired and not allowed to retire. Let some of the people in the employment lines who really need a job, work and take their place. The money they spent should have to be repaid by each person who attended. They should be billed for their airfare, hotel, food, entertainment, fortune teller and whatever else they had. A certain portion of each activity should be allocated to them.

If you really want to talk about entitlements, look at all your Senators, Congressmen, etc. They are the epitome of entitlements. Who else do you know have the benefits they are being given? They represent to me the definition of entitlements.

I once was told of a young lady on government assistance. I'm not sure if it was disability or what, but she was on some kind of assistance. To my knowledge she had never worked. The government found out they had supposedly underpaid her approximately $13,000.00 and sent her a check for this amount. If you have never paid into the system, how in the hell can you be underpaid?

People carrying other people children on their income tax, what the hell! Isn't there some way to track this? Can't we link the social security number at birth to the mother and issue that number before the baby leaves the hospital? Or maybe suggesting an original birth certificate each time a child is added onto your income tax? You should have people in place who are more knowledgeable than me and can figure out ways to thwart this fraud. There is fraud in every government agency, County and State Agency I would bet on it.

Then you have some people who hire their friends and pay them a tremendous salary, who in turn bring in their friends and pay them a high salary, all the while bypassing those who have been on the job for years. This happened on a Civil Services Job, and everyone is afraid to speak up.

SOCIAL SECURITY

First, let me tell you social security is <u>NOT</u> an entitlement. Years ago the government decided to sell social security insurance and it would pay out if you lived to a certain age or was disabled. We paid for social security insurance and we had no choice. It was mandatory that you participate. I was under the impression the government was putting this money in a fund so that it could grow, in order to pay us when we became of age or was disabled. Now you come up with a problem, but whose problem is it anyway, given we were forced to participate? I can understand it if you change the benefits for future recipients, give them a choice of whether to participate or not. But, those of us who have already paid into the system, we have no choice but to pay them social security. You can't change the rules once I'm in the game.

FIRST LADY MICHELLE OBAMA

Not only is she the first Black First Lady, she's also beautiful. Someone told me she gets more hate mail than her husband. Why? She has impeccable style and taste and always looks elegant. She has done a terrific job of highlighting the plight of our veterans and obesity, yet she is even criticized for some of that.

Rush Limbaugh simply seems to hate her. He reminds me of the Civil Rights era, when White men were rapping Blacks by day and raping Black women by night. Some of them even had wives, but they couldn't resist the Black woman. Personally, I think this is his problem. He is so enamored with Michelle Obama until he can't resist talking about her. My thought is he would love to have her himself, and is mad at himself for having those thoughts. This is the only explanation I can think of as to why he is so obsessed with Michelle Obama. I can hallucinate the same as him, right? As Bobby Brown sang "That's My Prerogative."

There was a time years ago when it was said the only two people that were free, was a White man and a Black woman. A White man could always have a Black woman and nothing was ever said or done about it, but a Black man had to hide if he had an interest in a White woman. She was like gold to him. I know people who had to leave our town because they were involved with a White woman, yet there were White men openly involved with Black women.

No one could possibly believe all the hatred Rush Limbaugh spews about President Obama and Michelle. He's gotten filthy rich doing this. I think he laughs at you idiots all the way to the bank, because you continue to believe him. I used to say racism is not going to end until all old timers die, but I apologize for being wrong. I personally don't think it will ever end.

All I can say about Mr. Limbaugh is to quote Proverbs 17:12, "Face a bear robbed of her cubs, but never a fool in his folly."

IGNORANCE CORNER

Sarah Palin questions the Christmas card highlighting the dog "Bo." Doesn't this woman have anything more to do with her time than to be so petty and jealous of the Obama's? I am sure they spend as much time on thoughts of her (smile). It's hard for me to believe the American public could be so gullible as to believe what she says, when she doesn't know shit from shinola. "Going Rogue." I'm sure if anybody knows anything about going rogue, it would certainly be her. To think she was almost Vice-President of the country gives you chills doesn't it? It does me. She is saying things some people want to hear, but she can't possibly believe all the ignorant misinformation she spews out of her mouth about President Obama. I will guarantee you she is laughing all the way to the bank about how easy it is to dupe you fools into spending money on her. How much is she worth now, in comparison to what she was worth when John McCain discovered her living in an outhouse in Alaska? This is my opinion only, and I have as much right to my opinion as she does.

Allen West was suggesting "get the hell out of the United States," too late Allen. We didn't ask to come here, but now that we have lost blood, sweat and tears helping make this country become what it is today, there is no way I'm going anywhere. I suppose you think you're something special. If the police should meet you and another Black person in similar circumstances, the results would be the same. You would be treated as a N---A the same as the other Black person, so shut the hell up and go on back to Africa. "I suppose he is one of Ann Coulter's "Our Blacks are so much better than their Blacks." He is an example of what I would call a N---A, and I don't like the word and do not use it, but in this instance I had to. No other word is appropriate. As my husband always say, "N----'S and flies, the only difference between them is one will shit on you and the other one will eat it."

Newt Gingrich wants to talk about food stamps. Can he give even one of those people on food stamps a J-O-B? Okay Newt, African Americans are demanding paychecks. What are you going to do? Not only are African Americans demanding jobs, but poor people in general are demanding jobs.

Mitt Romney is worth approximately $250 million dollars. How many jobs has he created in the last 5 years? They say the 1% create the jobs; how many have they created lately? Why hasn't he taken at least $200 million of it and started some type of company to put some people to work, if he's such a business minded person and cause celebre of working magic with companies. Who needs $250 million dollars in a lifetime? Your children should all be college educated and able to take care of themselves. I believe money is to be shared, not hoarded. So if the Lord has blessed you, you should also be a blessing to others. This is true morality and spirituality, to whom much is given much is expected. Yet the Republicans want to preach and teach morality and spirituality as if they invented it, when they are nothing more than hypocrites themselves. A wolf in sheep's clothing is the best description I can offer.

I think it is only fair to ask both presidential candidates to lay out a specific plan they envision for the next four years for the country. Don't just say revamp Medicare, social security and reduce the deficit, etc. Tell us exactly how you plan to do it. This way we can evaluate both plans before we have the opportunity to vote and decide who we think would be the best president for the next four years.

Rev. Jesse Lee Peterson would send Blacks back to the plantation. Who the f--k says we ever left the plantation? Slavery was supposed to have ended in the 1800's, but that's a lie. I was born in 1943 and Blacks in Louisiana were still in slavery to me. Anytime you were subjected to the inhumane treatment of your people as I was in the 1950's, this was still slavery. So, Rev. Peterson, if you want to go back to the plantation go right ahead; only know hell no I'm not going! News Flash! Not only Black women are having babies out of wedlock, but all nationalities are having babies out of wedlock. You can't have it your way with abstinence, no abortion and no contraception. You Republicans are delusional if you think these young people are going to abstain from sex or not using various forms of contraception.

Proverbs 26:22 says "The words of a talebearer are like dainty morsels that sink into one's inmost being."

Louisiana Congressman John Fleming says he only has $400,000.00 after paying his bills etc. Boo hoo hoo! My heart bleeds for him. What do you tell the voters who only has $4 or nothing left after paying their bills? If he has $400,000 left, that means in 10 years he has amassed $4 Million dollars in savings.

Dick Cheney saying the President "has been unmitigated disaster to this country." Well so much for hopes and dreams. I had hoped a new heart would help Mr. Cheney, but I was wrong. The President might have been unmitigated disaster to this country, but at least he didn't shoot his hunting buddy.

BRISTOL PALIN

What can I say about Bristol? She reminds me of a joke I once received in an email. When you're covered and warm, even though it's in a pile of shit, keep your mouth closed. When you're living in a glass house, you can't afford to throw stones. So she disagreed with President Obama's stance on gay marriage, who asked her for any input? At least the magic word here is marriage, which she wouldn't know anything about. Her main claim to fame is being an unwed mother at the age of 18, and having a mother who is duping you idiots all the way to the bank. How much is she worth now in comparison to what she was worth when John McCain picked her to run on his ticket? She owes a debt of gratitude to Senator John McCain for being the one who brought her to the country's attention. I know Bristol didn't have the audacity to say, "We know that in general kids do better growing up in a mother/father home. Ideally, fathers help shape their kids worldview." Really Bristol!

What are we saying? Aren't we sending the wrong message to underage, unmarried parents when we reward them for such behavior? That brings to mind a comment my parent's used to make, "It's not always what you know, it's who you know." Her being rewarded with a reality show proves the point perfectly. How many young ladies have had babies at a young age and still went on to graduate from college? These are the young women we should be celebrating, not Bristol. What has she done? What kind of skill does it take to lie on your back and open your legs? My great niece went to college with three kids, worked a full time job and had a no good husband. She graduated from Santa Clara University with a B.S. in Psychology, had another baby, went on to UC Berkeley and graduated with her Master' Degree in Social Welfare, hoping to someday become a licensed therapist. These are the women we should be celebrating and saluting, women who have gone on to make something of their lives despite the obstacles. Life really is a tripp for some of us.

MY IDEAS ON KEEPING THE COUNTRY SAFE

Do you wanna know what really pisses me off; officials speaking about events anonymously? If you have not been authorized to speak, keep your damn mouth closed. Some people can't keep water on their stomach. We talk too much about what we are doing. The public does not need to know every aspect of what you are doing to keep the country safe. We need to learn the definition of a secret and follow it.

It's going to take all of us being more neighborly with our neighbors. We have to be more vigilant, conscientious and observant of our surroundings. We are so wrapped up with our own lives that we don't pay attention to our surroundings, but everyone has a part to play. We can't expect the government to do everything without our help.

The ways in which we are not doing what we should to protect the country, should not be divulged on national television. Don't they know or care that Al Qaida members or wanna be's might be watching? It's like my mother used to say "If the sense they had was in a woodpeckers head, he'd fly ass backwards."

MICHAEL VICK

Everyone wants to condemn this man for what he did. I say he that is without sin, let him cast the first stone. Sure he was wrong for what he did, but did he deserve jail time? Hell no! Everyone thinks dogs are so precious. Well whenever you mention dogs, all the image conjures up for me is a picture of the Policeman holding dogs and water hose to intimidate Black folks during the Civil Rights struggle. What would have been more effective? To have him do jail time or forfeit his salary for that same period of time as his incarceration and donate it to the Humane Society?

When White women picked up their maids, the dog was in the front seat with her and the maid was in the back seat. When the tight shoe is on your foot, you are the one uncomfortable and miserable. So, unless you've walked a mile in my shoes, don't tell me how I'm supposed to feel.

We have all got to learn how to live together in peace and harmony.

OCTOMOM

Well, it finally had to happen; the Octomom had to go on welfare. I'd pick shit with the chickens before I would resort to food stamps, placing my responsibility on someone else. I know it is not the children's fault they are in this predicament, nor is it the American people fault. She made a conscious, deliberate, and calculated decision to have all these babies with no way to take care of them. That's her problem. She has to learn for each decision you make, there are consequences that goes along with it. We would love to have had 3 or 4 children, but financially we felt we could only afford two and that is what we had. All those right wingers, the doctor and pro-life groups should be forced to take care of the children. This is truly when you see how hypocritical they are. Has anyone stepped forward to support her children? Hell no!

OUR CHILDREN

I think the whole country has gone completely mad. There are numerous hideous crimes committed against our children. With all the pain and suffering some of our children experience in their short life time, it would have been better if they were never born. Just because a woman has a womb does not mean she has to have an embryo in it. All women are not mothers and all mothers are not women.

What has or is happening with our children and the violence in some of them? As far as I'm concerned, our troops should not be in Afghanistan or Iraq. They should be patrolling the streets of some of our most violent areas, such as Chicago, etc. They have taken too many innocent children and other people lives with their violence.

DEATH PENALTY

There has been talk lately of abolishing the death penalty. I am not sure about that. If the defendant is caught like the gunman in the Aurora, Colorado killings moments after the shooting dressed in full riot gear, 3 weapons, an AR15 Assault Rifle, a Remington 12 Gauge shotgun and a .40 Glock handgun, there should be no innocent until proven guilty. You are guilty without a doubt, what other evidence do you need? He was caught with unmistakable proof he is guilty. It was premeditated, and there is no doubt he is guilty. Once they have been given the death penalty, it should take effect immediately. They should not be on death row longer than one year. Why should the citizens have to pay the rest of their life for food, housing, clothing and medical expenses, etc. for the prisoner? But we always want to be so fair, let justice prevail, etc. To hell with that scenario! The Lord really has to change my heart, because I'm not there yet. If you're a parent or relative and know Uncle Joe or your child is crazy or has the potential of hurting someone, it is your responsibility to alert someone. Also, if they are this crazy it would put them out of their misery and keep the public safe. For anyone this crazy, imagine the pain they must be feeling.

Obviously, I like the theory a life for a life. If you kill someone on purpose, not by accident with the obvious intent of seeing them dead, you are guilty in my book. It's like the theory in some Islamic countries. If you steal, they cut off your hand. My theory is if the offenders knew the consequences of their actions and knew they were going to be dealt with swift action, there would be less inclination to do these horrendous crimes.

POVERTY TOUR

I never really understood the benefits of the poverty tour. Did anyone receive anything valuable such a job, monetary award, voter registration etc. from this poverty tour? It doesn't take Einstein to figure out that a lot of us are living in poverty. We see instances of that every day on the news. Tavis Smiley alone is worth over $10 million dollars. I don't know how much Cornel West is worth, but I'm sure it is equally as much or more than Tavis.

If I was worth approximately $10 to 20 million dollars, I wouldn't just have a tour, I'd spread some of my wealth around. What difference does it make whether you call it a poverty tour, po' folks tour or ain't go no money tour. After all, who needs $10 million dollars? My belief is money is to be shared with the less fortunate; it is not to be hoarded. You have never seen a Brink's Armored truck following a hearse after the funeral. I used to have great respect and admiration for both Tavis and Cornel, but I have lost it for both of them with all the foolishness spewing out of their mouths.

What I am about to say is not going to win me any friends or a popularity contest. The fact is, I would be totally remiss if I didn't mention the fact that some African-Americans need to do more to help ourselves. Some of us could have had a PhD as long as we have been sitting around crying about the lack of jobs. We need to look at where the demand for jobs are and concentrate on entering those fields. The field of Computers and Computer Technology are wide open. They are begging for qualified applicants so much so that they are importing people from other countries. How many African-Americans did you see become instant millionaires with the advent of Facebook going public?

It is imperative for us to get off the sidelines and become more tech savvy in the 21st Century. We have all the latest and greatest electronic gadgets known to man;

cell phones, I Pad, I Phone, Nook, and Kindle, etc. Yet, we are not having any impact in these two fields. Why? My mom used to preach the value of an education, even though she had none. She was considered illiterate because she could not read nor write. She signed her name with a X. What she lacked in education, she more than made up for with mother wit (common sense).

Her motto was, "You should do better than we did. Your children should do better than you did. This is how you break the chains of poverty." So far, we have done as she suggested. I did well in school, but couldn't afford to go to college. However, I did finish high school and was able to secure decent jobs in my work life. We had two children. Both graduated from college. One graduated from Morris Brown College in Atlanta, GA. and the other one graduated from UC Berkeley. Now, they are both self-sufficient and have good jobs.

SAME-SEX MARRIAGE

My position on this issue is slowly evolving as the President's. I have never been against this issue all along. My main issue was having to change the definition of marriage after all those years. I completely agree that same sex couples and transgendered individuals should have the same rights as married heterosexuals. I would have had no objections to changing whatever federal laws that had to be changed to allow these couples to have the same rights and privileges as heterosexual couples. For example, if they called themselves life partners (for lack of a better word), the definition would be the union between same-sex couples or transgendered individuals. That would allow them to be married and have all rights and privileges of a married couple. Only couples who go through this procedure would be eligible, not people living together. This should satisfy both gays and religious leaders without infringing on anybody's beliefs. What do we lose as a result of this law? Nothing.

Who are we to say their lifestyle is wrong? We shouldn't be judging anyone. Only God can judge and each of us has to see God for ourselves. I am sick and tired of all the debating that goes on about this issue when all along the solution should have been a simple one. To me, this would be more palatable to many people than changing the definition of marriage. Some in Congress will never agree to this. As my mother used to say, "You catch more flies with honey than you do with vinegar," and "There's more than one way to skin a cat" or "When you got your hand in the lion's mouth, you can't snatch it out; you have to ease it out."

If I had a choice today, I would vote for Gay Marriage, but I know some of those "holier than thou" members of Congress will never agree to this.

PRESIDENT BARACK OBAMA

Disrespect

I don't know how this man keeps his cool at all times. He had been ridiculed, disrespected, talked about, defamed and you name it and it has been done to him. You don't have to like him, but the office of our President should be respected. It's just like our boss on a job; we don't have to like him or her, but we should have respect for the position he or she has been placed in.

I can't understand why the President doesn't tout his accomplishments on his watch. It's okay to be modest, but not to be afraid to declare what has been accomplished on your watch. They include:

1. Affordable Health Care Act

2. Saved the automakers. (What was Mitt Romney's response "let them fail" thereby creating more chaos for many families.)

3. Got Osama Bin Laden and a bunch of his buddies (allies).

4. Repealed don't ask, don't tell.

5. Credit card statements for the first time indicate how much interest and time it takes to pay off if you pay only the minimum due.

6. Nominated Sonia Sotomayor and Elena Kagan to the Supreme Court.

7. Signed the Lilly Ledbetter Fair Pay Act in 2009.

8. Authorized the Navy Seals to secure the release of a U. S. Captain held by Somali pirates and ordered increased patrols off the coast.

9. These are just a few of his accomplishments, there are others.

Personally, I think he is the kind of man who doesn't want to brag about his successes because the economy is still struggling, and he knows it has to be fixed. For example, his decision to not get involved in arming the Rebels in Syria is spot on, because how do you know who or what you are arming? The first nation all countries in conflict call upon is the United States, but before and afterwards they hate our guts. Why can't some of the other countries take the lead sometimes? Why does it always fall on us? We are still committed to Afghanistan. How can we afford the financial burden, and why should we send our young men and women to put their lives on the line?

With the money we have spent on Iraq and Afghanistan, we could have saved most, if not all the homeowners whose homes were under water or foreclosed on.

The thought of a Black man running the country is just too much for a lot of people to comprehend, especially the old timers. It just drives them out of their minds; never mind the fact that this country has existed all these years with White men controlling the country, no matter what kind of a job they did. He was White and that is all that mattered. Never have we had anyone smarter, more articulate, caring, professional, handsome, and more willing to admit when he makes a mistake or believes in this country. He is constantly criticized for whatever he does; he can't do or say anything right for some people. He just let it roll off his back, like water off a duck's back. I couldn't or wouldn't do it.

ECONOMY

Mitt Romney talks a lot about the economy, but have you heard him give any specifics on how he would get more jobs in America? Talk is cheap! Anyone can talk, but that's just all it is. Suppose you elect him and he is unable to create any more jobs than the present President, then what do you do? He will soon find out the President does not create jobs. Employers, companies and people create jobs. What really irritates me is when you call certain companies about a problem, the individual who answers your call is located in another country. They don't have the slightest idea what you are talking about, if you are even lucky enough to understand what they are saying to you.

I remember a specific problem I had with a United Airlines representative located in another country. I was a United Airlines retiree and had a problem with my luggage. I had attempted to fly space available and was unsuccessful. It seems my luggage made the flight, but I didn't. So after several days of not receiving my luggage, I called. The person who answered did not even know what I meant by the term SA (space available). Can you imagine my frustration trying to explain to her what a SA was? This should've been common knowledge for someone working for them.

Richard Cebull, Montana's Chief Federal Judge, forwarded an email comparing African-Americans to dogs and insinuating the President's mother had sex with animals. This is where I draw the line. You don't talk about my momma and I won't talk about yours. These are fighting words when said to most Black people. He issued an apology but he wouldn't have had to issue me an apology, because I would have whipped his natural white ass until he turned Black as me. But then that is the difference between the President and me, class.

Proverbs 15:14 says "The mind of the intelligent man seeks knowledge, but the mouth of fools feed on folly."

The birther controversy, can you believe how much time and energy has been lost on this debate alone? I don't give a damn where he was born. All I know is he is my President now, and I will treat him with the same respect I have treated all of our other Presidents. Aren't all presidential candidates supposed to be vetted. Whose responsibility is this? If he was born in another country, this is not his problem; too bad, so sad; it is too late now. Get over it! It's a funny thing, this has been a non-issue for forty-three presidents, and all of a sudden there is a problem. There is one thing I will have to applaud our former President Bush for, and that is keeping himself above the fray.

A MEMBER OF CONGRESS YELLING OUT "YOU LIE!"

Donald Trump! I wouldn't vote for dogcatcher! He thought he could actually run the country and some of you idiots did too. I have only one thing to say about him, and that is Proverbs 26:11 says "As a dog returns to his vomit, so the fool repeats his folly."

Arizona Governor Jan Brewer pointing her finger in the President's face, should've been me. Woman or not, she disrespected me. She deserved anything she would have gotten, including slapping her hand out of my face. Who does she think she is, treating the President of the United States like you would when you scold a child?

Congressman Joe Walsh announcing he wouldn't attend the President's September 8, 2011 speech. La-de-da! Way to go Congressman. Did you miss his presence? I did; I cried all night because he wasn't there.

Senate Minority Leader Mitch McConnell, in December 2010, announced his top political priority over the next two years would be to deny President Obama a second term. Instead of pledging to work with him to the benefit of the country, he's telling all voters who voted for this man, "F—k you and what you want! This is what I am going to do. You can like it or lump it."

Charles and David Koch and 250-300 of their friends pledged about 100 million dollars to defeat President Obama in the election, come on let's help them lose that $100 million dollars, they can afford it.

SOLYANDRA

It wouldn't surprise me if there was some sort of sabotage going on in this instance. How can you have such a perfect plan in place on paper and not execute it. This may have been done intentionally to embarrass the President.

However, someone from this group should be in jail and doing hard time, because something had to happen to all the money given to them. I'll bet the leader and its board of directors are living in fat city and laughing all the way to the bank at what a fool it made of the President.

Robert Friess was saying something to the fact that "I hope his teleprompters are bullet proof." Isn't this the s—t you've come to expect from the Republicans?

Allen West, imitating a large number of Democrats are Communist. They just flat out lie and not one of the Republicans has the balls to call them out on their lies.

If the 99% vote for Mitt Romney and his 1% rich friends, you deserve everything that happens to you. You have to be careful of what you wish for. You know what you have; you don't know what you're getting. You can see who's backing the Republican candidate; the utterly ridiculous rich. For what reason other than to buy the Presidency? They already have everything money can buy; now they want the power. Now they're out to prove to the 99% they can buy the Presidency also, thanks to your not so Supreme Court ruling to allow corporations to give unlimited money to influence election results.

Gretchen Carlson criticizing Jimmy Fallon for calling the President "Prezzy of the United Steezy." Is she for real? He has been called everything but a child of God by her fellow Repugs. Now she wants to say he represents the highest office of the land, the most important figure in the world and going on comedy shows lowers the state of the office. She and her fellow Repugs disrespect him every chance they get, yet they have the audacity to expect respect from a bunch of radicals. Give me a fuck . . . g break? Doesn't she know the people who attend comedy shows vote and should be represented too? The President should go wherever he needs in order to talk to the people. She should disclose these facts to her fellow colleagues. It never ceases to amaze me about the ignorance and double talking coming from them. This isn't McDonald's! You can't have it your way. It is fine for you to show disrespect for the office of the President, and this leads others to the same disrespect. You can't expect respect from others, when all you or your partners in crime have shown is total disrespect for the office.

There are just a few articles of disrespect shown to the President of the United States. There are many more, but you get the gist of what I'm saying.

The Republicans would have you to believe the rich create jobs; how ludicrous. How many jobs has Mitt Romney created with his $250 million dollars? Those remodeling his house do not count. Where do they expect to spend eternity? They are so religious and self-righteous. One thing I can say unequivocally and without a doubt; death is the equalizer. No matter how rich or poor you are, we are all going to die. There will be no more lying and distorting the facts. It reminds me of a joke someone sent me in an email. I don't know the source, but I've included a copy here for your perusal.

An old country preacher had a teenage son. It was getting time the boy should give some thought to choosing a profession. Like many young men his age, the boy didn't really know what he wanted to do, and he didn't seem too concerned about it. One day, while the boy was away at school, his father decided to try an experiment. He went into the boy's room and placed on his study table four objects.

1. A Bible . . .

2. A silver dollar . . .

3. A bottle of whiskey . . .

4. And a Playboy magazine . . .

"I'll just hide behind the door," the old preacher said to himself. "When he comes home from school today, I'll see which object he picks up.

If it's the Bible, he's going to be a preacher like me, and what a blessing that would be.

If he picks up the dollar, he's going to be a business man, and that would be okay too.

But if he picks up the bottle, he's going to be a no-good drunken bum, and Lord, what a shame that would be.

And worse of all, if he picks up that magazine he's going to be a skirt-chasing womanizer.

The old man waited anxiously, and he soon heard his son's footsteps as he entered the house whistling and headed for his room.

The boy tossed his books on the bed. As he turned to leave the room, he spotted the objects on the table.

With curiosity in his eyes, he walked over to inspect them. Finally, he picked up the Bible and placed it under his arm. He picked up the silver dollar and dropped it into his pocket. He uncorked the bottle and took a big drink, while he admired this month's centerfold.

"Lord have mercy," the old preacher disgustedly whispered.

"HE'S GONNA RUN FOR Congress."

Still another joke sent to me by one of my friends is the following one. I do not know with whom or where this joke originated, but here it goes.

It just dawned on me!!

My dog sleeps about 20 hours a day. He has his food prepared for him. He can eat whenever he wants.

His meals are provided at no cost to him. He visit the doctor once a year for his checkup, and again during the year if any medical needs arise.

For this he pays nothing, and nothing is required of him.

He lives in a nice neighborhood in a house that is much larger than he needs, but he is not required to do any upkeep. If he make a mess, someone else cleans it up.

He has his choice of places to sleep. He receives these accommodations absolutely free.

He is living like a king, and has no expenses whatsoever.

All of his cost are picked up by others who go out and earn a living every day.

I was just thinking about all this, and suddenly it hit me like a brick . . .

I THINK MY DOG IS A MEMBER OF CONGRESS!

Frankly, I am not convinced that losing the election would be the worst thing that could happen to President Obama or his family. Let me explain. He has the burden of carrying millions of people on his back, some of who are ungrateful people, trying to save them from themselves by doing what he thinks is best or more beneficial to them and their families. President Obama does not need the people, the people need him, because he and his family are going to be fine from a financial point of view regardless of whether he is President or not. It will not take any hair off his back; it would take a lot of the stress and worry off him. My illiterate mom used to say all the time, "Don't cut off your nose to spite your face." Yet that is precisely what a lot of you poor people are doing. You can't see the forest for the trees. Some of you "don't have a pot to piss in or a window to throw it out of."

Frankly, I think a lot of businesses are sitting on a pile of cash refusing to hire, just waiting and hoping for a Romney win. If he does win, I expect them to start hiring to insinuate that it is because of Mitt Romney.

Go ahead and elect a Republican! He will give you the worst ass whipping you have ever had, and you will deserve it. So go ahead and take that ass whipping. Just remember, you had a choice. I recently read where 40% of you West Virginian's voted for an inmate in a Texas prison over the President. Good for you! You West Virginian's who are poor as Jobs turkey. He shitted and didn't have nothing left. I guess you thought we'll show him; why should he continue to try and convince people what is in their best interest? The President has enough education, money and ability to make even more money to take care of his family for their lifetime. To hell with trying to save people from themselves!

This reminds me of a situation that happened years ago. A young man across the street from my friend was beating his wife, and my friend hollers across the street "leave her alone!" Later on the wife comes across the street to my friend's house and says to her something similar to this, "When my man is whipping my ass, you stay out of it!" Well, that's the same way I feel about this situation; everybody should stay out of it. I would be so quiet, you could hear a rat pissing on cotton.

<u>RACISM</u>

So, racism is supposedly dead. Who told that lie and that is what it is, "a lie." I used to say "racism will end when all of us old timers die off, but I was wrong. Racism will never die! Racism is alive, well and thriving in the United States. I am not always one who sees every incident as racism, but I do see the articles I referenced below as racist.

The murder of Trayvon Martin was as cold, calculated and premeditated as you can call it. I don't understand how anyone can say otherwise. Take into consideration the following facts we know to be true:

1. George Zimmerman was out of his vehicle, and did follow Trayvon.

2. Trayvon was in a gated community.

3. He was never asked for identification.

4. He wasn't asked do you live here or are you visiting someone who lives here?

5. The police asked him not to follow this young man. He disobeyed a Police directive.

6. The Neighborhood Watch Group was supposedly never sanctioned.

7. Why was a Neighborhood Watch person carrying a 9mm gun, unless he was intending to use it? All the Neighborhood Watch groups I know of just watch and report. Why was this one so different?

8. Suppose he had been the one burglarizing the neighborhood. Burglary vs. murder? Which one is the more permanent one. Is it worth it to take a life over a simple burglary? You can always get more things, but you can't replace a life. Once it's taken, you can never give it back. A blind person can see through this facade.

Newt Gingrich asking for President Obama to denounce De Niro for his remarks about the country not being ready for a White first lady; did he denounce Paula Smith for making the bumper sticker "Don't Re-Nig in 2012?" What De Niro said pales in comparison to what she said. If she had meant truly not to offend anyone, she would've used "Don't Re-Neg in 2012" being short for "Don't Re-Nege in 2012." She knew exactly what she was saying was what most conservatives wanted to hear. If she says differently, she's telling a bald face lie. Her statement, "I have kids here around me that are Black kids, I call them my own." Whoop de do; that cliche really gets to me whenever it is used! I have friends who are Black or kids. I don't recall ever referring to my White friends in this way. I have some of the best White friends you could ever encounter. I never ever refer to them as my White friends, they are simply referred to as my friends.

Can you imagine Geraldo Rivera saying the hoodie was the problem, not George Zimmerman? If he feels the hoodie was the problem, he may as well blame the manufacturer of the hoodie for Trayvon's death. What an ignoramus! I stopped listening to anything Geraldo had to say when his rants against O. J. Simpson were so animated. He was so incensed, you would have thought he actually saw O. J. doing the killing of Nicole and Ron. That's one reason I got so pissed at O. J. in Las Vegas. He knew they were waiting for him to make one false move to arrest him, yet he goes into Las Vegas and acts like "Mr. Big Stuff." They should have gotten him for stupidity alone.

You have individuals committing murder and do not receive the sentence O. J. was given. That is how you know they were out to get him for anything they could. He played right into their hands. Now you have renowned investigator William Dear who says O. J. is innocent; his son did the killing. There are contrasting views between O. J. and Trayvon's death. In O. J.'s case, when the jury found him not guilty most people were appalled. Yet in Trayvon's case, they want you to let justice prevail. Do we have two systems of justice in this country? Are we supposed to?

Frank Taafe says Trayvon should have acted accordingly. What does he mean accordingly to what? All George Zimmerman had to do was ask the teenager did he live there or where was he going. He could have followed the teenager to where he was going. George Zimmerman should have been charged with disobeying a police directive if nothing else. Why should we always have to drill our children on what to do and how to react in certain conditions, if everyone is to be treated equally. I try to tell my son and grandson how to react, but some things you may forget.

If everyone wasn't so busy watching our kids, they may have caught Bernie Madoff before he ruined so many people lives with his Ponzi scheme. Everyone is so busy watching Black children steal a few dollars and the

White man or woman is stealing the whole damn store. Who are most of your embezzlers; people who steal from their employers, etc.?

I won't even repeat the stupid statement Glenn Beck made. I was dumfounded.

THE CATHOLIC CHURCH AND CONTRACEPTION

So the Catholic Church is up in arms about providing coverage for women who want to have insurance that covers contraception? Why should that be news to us? That's a part of their responsibility. If they don't want this provision covered by insurance, why don't they only hire workers who think and agree with them?

Do they authorize Viagra or Cialis? I feel a woman has a right to decide what she can handle and what she cannot. I was under the impression there is supposed to be separation of church and state. If the Catholic Church is naive enough to think all those brides wearing white are not having premarital sex before marriage, then I'd like to talk to them about selling them the Golden Gate Bridge, and I don't even own it. You cannot convince me the women aren't using contraception and having plenty of sex.

In an article published in everyday health, it stated teen birth rates tend to be higher in right-swinging/

conservative states. Is that a fact? The more conservative the state, the higher the teen birth rate. Conservative kids have less sex, I suppose. Is that what we're saying? Let's not fool ourselves.

The Republicans are nothing more than hypocrites. They want to force women to have babies, but their obligation stops at birth. They want to do nothing at all to help mother's take care of their children once they are here; no food stamps or housing. They ought to be forced to take care of the children after birth.

Bishop Daniel Jenky comparing the President policies to Hitler and Stalin, I know he didn't go there did he? Bishop Jenky is quoted as having a calculated disdain of the President of the United States. I have a calculated disdain for the number of Catholic Priest who molested little boys for years and fathered children. Is he proud of that? I haven't heard his disdain for something as horrific as taking these children's innocence. He has the audacity to criticize the President, and he "can't pour piss out of a boot, if the directions say turn me down."

REPUBLICIANS vs. DEMOCRATS

Contrary to Mr. Herman Cain and Pat Buchanan's belief, we Blacks are not a monolithic group. We have minds of our own and are independent of one another.

As quiet as it is kept, we Liberals do have some thoughts and agreement with some conservative views. The thing that separates the Liberals from the Conservatives, is that we Liberals tend to be non-judgmental whereas the Conservatives are just the opposite. They are judgmental and it's their way or no way. If you're not in agreement with their position then you are wrong.

When you have a baby, that is your choice and decision. The government should not have to help you. If we had never started helping with your first child, maybe you wouldn't have had more. My husband and I decided we could only support two children, and that is what we had. I come from a large family of eight (8) children, so we would have loved to have had more. But unfortunately, because we felt it was our responsibility to have only as many as we could afford to properly take care of, we only had two.

I can remember the time if you were on welfare, the social workers came to your house trying to catch a man there. They had better not find a man at your house. My father hunted, fished and gigged for frogs to help support his family. I can remember my brother use to help my father with the frogs and they used to sell them. My brother sold so many frogs until they used to call him froggie. None of that mattered because we were never hungry, and nobody ever gave us anything. When I came to California, I was shocked to learn that frogs were considered a delicacy.

The government should help with your first child, and for a certain period of time only. They should not continue to help as you lie around and have baby after baby; some you know who the father is and some you don't. After the first baby, you're on your own. This may sound heartless, but maybe you would've stopped after one if you were not being supported by the taxpayers. For each decision we make, there are consequences and you should have taken that into account. I feel sorry for the children, but it was your decision only. My husband watches Maury Povich sometimes, and I am amazed. Some women test 9 or 10 men, and none of them are the father of the child. What does this say about the mother? What do you tell your child? This is a disgrace and so unfair to the children. I didn't realize there were so many children living a lifestyle where the mother does not know who the child's father is. Just when I think he couldn't possibly find any more of these women, he comes up with another group.

On the other hand, Conservatives believe in pro-life, but refuse to help you when the baby is born. They should be forced to take care of that baby from birth to adulthood. They don't even want you to practice birth control; how asinine is that? I guarantee you if they have unmarried young sons or daughters, they are having plenty of sex and practicing birth control. They may fool their parent's, but they can't fool the public. We are not naive enough or want to fool ourselves into believing this is true.

Medicare and Medicaid should be revamped; there is a lot of waste in these programs. It is because there is a lot of fraud that goes on with the consumers, doctors, and hospitals, etc. I have a friend who is of Vietnamese descent and his mother had a light stroke. She had been transferred to a place for rehab, only they weren't doing a very good job of rehabilitation. He came in one day and the stench of urine in the room was so strong until he couldn't stand it. He had to empty his mom's commode as well as his mom's roommate, so what are they being paid for? And for this, they were charging the government $2,300.00 per day.

Also Amanda Clayton winning one million dollars in the lottery and still collecting welfare. She has bills to pay! Hell, so do I, and I haven't won the lottery! If her bills total more than $1 million dollars, that's her fault and her problem. With that amount of money, she should be able to live a very modest lifestyle for the remainder of her life. Anytime someone wins the lottery, they should never again be given public assistance. It is not the voters fault or problem if they squandered all the money they won. We don't owe them anything. I find that most people buy what they want and beg for what they need. For example, $109 to $150 for Michael Jordan tennis shoes. Mike should be ashamed to align his name with something so expensive. It's not like he's starving or really need the money.

While we are on the subject, it is not our problem to help some people. I don't care how many babies you have, as long as the taxpayers are not expected to help take care of them. If you have 8, 9, 10 babies, etc. without a husband to help you, you should have figured out before hand how you are going to take care of them. It is unfair to place this burden on the backs of taxpayers, or to put your children in this position. There are some people who are genuinely trying to take care of their families and are having problems. Those people need help from us, and Mitt Romney or Rick Santorum who do not believe in contraception.

I cannot believe Mitt Romney is not worried about the poor. Does he think they enjoy being poor all their lives and don't have aspirations that one day they will live normal lives and not have to rob Peter to pay Paul? Of course, a man worth approximately 250 million dollars cannot identify with someone who makes maybe $12,000.00 a year or less. These people and their standard of living is so beneath him. Yet some of the poorest people vote Republican. It is beyond my comprehension.

Ann Romney with contempt and disdain saying "you people", who was her intended audience? I know she didn't mean "me." Her husband is running for President; if he didn't want to release this information maybe he shouldn't have put his hat in the ring. "If you can't stand the heat, stay out of the kitchen." This request should not have come as a surprise to him or her. This is something all prospective candidates do and have been doing for some years.

Do you want Rick Santorum running the country according to his religious beliefs? Who died and left him in charge and said his religious convictions were perfect? I know a lot of so called Christians who talk that talk, but can they walk that walk? Christianity reveals itself in the ways you treat your fellow men and women, not by what you say. You shouldn't have to go around telling people you are a Christian. It should be manifested in your everyday life.

A few weeks ago, I was talking to some young folks. They had a very interesting theory. They believed America is becoming more like a third world country, where you have the rich enclosed behind walls and fences and the poor folks on the other side. I certainly hope this does not happen, but it is a real possibility.

Also you have some of the very rich give up their US Citizenship in order to avoid taxes. Fine, but they should be forced to leave the country the very next day after the announcement. If they do not want to be here, we don't want to keep them any longer than necessary. They should never again be allowed in the US, not even to visit. If they have made most of their fortune while here, they should be made to pay a penalty with no exception being made.

My husband and I are fans of westerns, both old and new. A few weeks ago, there was a Cheyenne Marathon starring Clint Walker on TV. It reminded me so of the turmoil and conflict going on in Congress today, the same as was portrayed at that time, but it was fictional. It seems Cheyenne had gone to Congress to lobby for a specific cause. There was a Congressman there who continued to stonewall and filibuster any attempt by him to speak. Finally, one participant in the courtroom after seeing all this, made the statement the reason this Congressman was against this particular bill, was because he had an investment in this venture himself, and he also told about the lies this Congressman had told on another member. I thought dejavu! This is almost the same as it is today and it's not fictional. This aired somewhere between 1955 and 1963. The show was the first hour long western.

I cannot believe the money being donated for the Presidential race. Romney is alleged to have raised $35 Million dollars more in June than President Obama. Frightening isn't it! The mere fact that the President of the United States can be bought and paid for by the very rich; yet these are the same people who holler like a stuck pig, or object to paying their fair share of the tax burden. Yet the 99% of us refuse to believe or are too lackadaisical to even go to the polls and vote. They're not interested in us.

If the Presidency is won on the fact of who raises the most money, we are in a real quagmire and democracy as we once knew it is gone forever. There is no way in hell for a presidential candidate who is trying to do the right thing, to keep pace with the Super Political Action Committee (PAC), millionaires and billionaires who can give unlimited amounts of cash. You can thank the Supreme Court for our loss of democracy. There is no way in hell to keep pace with the donations of the 1%, when you represent the 99%. They do not have the resources to donate at the same rate.

Now that the Supreme Court has upheld the Affordable Care Act, when is Rush Limbaugh leaving the country? I wonder if he needs help packing for his departure. With Justice Roberts voting the way he did, it gives me some minor hope that the court is not all about politics. There should be a pledge given and taken by all members of the Supreme Court to denounce all affiliation with their particular party and govern strictly by the Constitution, not their philosophical views. Think of the hunting trip Justice Scalia took with Vice-President Dick Cheney. No one on the Supreme Court should have that close of a relationship with the Vice-President; it could give us the illusion of a conflict of interest. This is a lifetime appointment and the public needs to have some assurance that politics will in no way influence the members of the court.

The Republicans are up in arms about this ruling on this particular issue. I don't recall seeing this outrage when the court allowed unlimited campaign contributions by corporations. Did I miss something? I don't understand the hypocrisy of some individuals, nor the reasoning behind this decision. I didn't hear a peep coming from the conservatives. They were so quiet you could "hear a rat pissing on cotton."

Instead of the Republicans declaring to work with the Democrats to strengthen this plan, all they say is "we will work to repeal." In all the years this country has been in existence there was never a plan for healthcare. Why? Now all of a sudden you're going to work to repeal and replace it with what? Do you have a plan for the poor, uninsured and students? You don't need healthcare; you can afford the best money can buy.

THERE OUGHTA BE A LAW

There oughta be a law against defiling a dead person name. How many times do we have to endure people writing books about a person after they are dead and gone? Apparently too many times, and people ask what is their motive? I'll tell you the motive, MONEY! Especially if the person they are talking about is a well-known figure. Today I was listening to the View, and they were discussing a woman who allegedly had an affair with John Kennedy. John Kennedy has been dead for almost forty nine (49) years, and she waits until now to write this trash. Does she have any empathy for his family? He is not here to dispute what she has to say. How would she feel if this was done to a member of her family or to her? At 19, did she know right from wrong? If not, that is a testament to her values and morals and how she was raised. Did anyone put a gun to her head and make her do the things she says she did to him or his friend? It is too bad the American people like to believe all the garbage they are fed. I would not give them a nickel for anything written about a person once they are deceased.

MORTGAGE TAXES

I was listening to CBS this morning. They were discussing how we were going to pay for the payroll tax credit. They thought it was unfair to be hidden in a new or refinanced mortgage loan. How much is it and what is the big deal? You're damned if you do and damned if you don't. You're supposed to identify how you are going to pay for programs upfront without adding to the deficit. Did I understand something wrong? Supposedly this was a very small charge monthly for the life of the loan. First, in my way of thinking those who purchase or refinance are getting a double bonus. You are not only getting the payroll tax credit, but also this cost is rolled into the interest rate, which means it is deductible as mortgage expense. I don't have a degree, a PhD or Doctorate, just mother wit (common sense), and if more of us had it we wouldn't be so quick to jump to a conclusion.

LIFE INSURANCE

This is another necessary evil if you are poor. Rarely do we have money to bury our loved one, so consequently we have to pay for life insurance. As poor as we were, our parents always maintained a small life insurance policy to bury us in the event something happened to us. As my sister-in-law says, "You don't want to have to holler twice, once because they are dead and the second time because you have no money to bury them with." It is a disgrace they were sold sick and accident policies instead of life insurance policies. Unfortunately most of them did not know that. When I retired from United Airlines, I took the life insurance policy I had with me. Little did I know the cost of this insurance would keep increasing as we aged. Before we were paying four hundred and seventy some dollars every six months for my husband's insurance. It doubled this year to $860.76 every six months, and when I inquired the representative told me it would increase again at age 75 to approximately $1,500.00.

Do they think us retirees are shitting money or what? Where do they expect us to get the additional money from? When each of us got our life insurance report in December 2011, my policy had a cash value of $646.45 and my husband's cash value was supposed to be $336.24 for a total of $982.69. Great I thought, because both our policy premiums were due, his for $860.76 and mine for $534.36 for a total of $1,395.12. I thought I would use the cash value to pay for his premium. That way I would only have to come up with the $534.36 for my premium. Boy was I ever wrong! By the time she got through figuring between the two of us, our cash value of $982.69 had dropped to a little over $235.71. To say I was shocked was an understatement. I was horrified and didn't understand any of it. Most insurance policies is a necessary evil for poor folks. If I had known this when I retired I could have gotten another insurance or saved the money we're paying in premiums for nine years.

The states have a racket going on, and it is a gold mine for them. When you check unclaimed money sources, there are a lot of people owed small sums of money. In order for you to claim these small amounts, it would cost you even more than the unclaimed money is. This way the states get to keep that money, because no one in their right mind is going to pay more than the unclaimed money is to get it. Instead, they should make a law if the unclaimed money is $500 or less, any next of kin should be able claim it. In some cases people are at the same address they have always lived at, yet it still winds up with the state. My uncle has a $100 and some dollars with the state of LA., and he has been dead for years; so what is the likelihood of someone claiming that money? My mother has roughly the same amount with the state. She's been deceased since 1986, and what is the likelihood of someone claiming this? I don't think any state makes any effort to find claimants or their families. There are millions of dollars the states are collecting interest on.

I.R.S.

Someone please tell me how do you get to owe the IRS millions of dollars, and owe them for a number of years? It seems to me there is a double standard being used in several areas. The first one being the amount of taxes millionaires pay in comparison to the common folks. Also if we owed the government $400 when we were working, there is no way we would have been allowed to owe them for years. If we hadn't made arrangements within six months' time for them to get their money, they would have garnished our check or account. Some kind of way, they would have gotten the money that was owed to the government, and I use six months, but I doubt they would have waited that long. So you tell me how do entertainers, sports stars, etc., get away with this practice for years and owe millions of dollars? Something has to be done about the middle class and taxes. You have a potential Presidential candidate running for President who doesn't even have to work, supposedly paying 13.9 percent tax on $250 million dollars, and you have some middle class taxpayers paying between 25% to 39% taxes on their working salaries. What is fair about this? All the Presidential nominee has to do is have the IRS release his adjusted gross income and the amount of taxes paid each year. No details are ever listed. If you have nothing to hide, prove you are not straight up lying. This is a simple solution.

TIGER WOODS

Yes, he was definitely wrong for cheating on his wife; but he who is without sin let them cast the first stone. When you're living in a glass house, you can't afford to throw stones. We have chastised and talked so mean about him, it is sacrilegious, he didn't kill or murder anyone. Whatever occurred is between him and his wife Elin. For the money she was paid, I am sure it is enough to help her heal the embarrassment, pain and hurt. I'd be crying all the way to the bank.

Don't you think there is a double standard going on here? On the other hand, we have former Governor Arnold Schwarzenegger, who years ago had an illegitimate child with his former housekeeper and kept it a secret for years. He stayed with his wife and family all those years living a lie. Now you tell me who the lowest form of humanity is. He probably had sex with the housekeeper in his wife's bed when she was away from the house. If he had balls big enough to tell himself it was okay to have sex with the housekeeper, why wouldn't he have the balls to screw her in his wife's own bed? Yet, there are those who are still crucifying Tiger years later, while the Governor is just a blip on the screen. I read some of your comments on the internet. It's almost as if we were better off without access to the internet. Some of us should never be allowed to use it. It is a shame that something so beautiful is used for so many of the wrong reasons. If I were Tiger, I'd tell everyone to kiss where the sun doesn't shine. He should have enough money to last a lifetime, even if he never wins another tournament, and if he doesn't that's his fault.

His former caddie should be grateful for the time he was blessed to be a part of Tiger's entourage. He paid him whatever they agreed upon, and now he is an ungrateful revengeful idiot. He was simply a bag toter. He never hit one ball for Tiger, made one birdie or hit one hole in one. He is like a teacher in the summertime "no class."

UNITED AIRLINES

This topic deals with United Airlines. I worked for them for 16+ years and a lot of others worked for them even longer. We gave up raises, lost our 401(k), and had the ESOP, and gave up numerous other benefits to help them survive. They filed bankruptcy and the PBGC had to take over paying their pensions. Now all of a sudden they have money for a whole rash of incentives for the current employees, including profit sharing without realizing or caring that it was the retirees who made United the brand it is today.

There oughta be a law that any company where the PBGC has had to take over, should have to pay back the money before there are any perks for current employees. The incentive should be the fact that you still have a job, which should be incentive enough for the employees, and if they don't perform they should be fired. That's my opinion, what's yours?

WHITNEY HOUSTON

I am still mourning the loss of Whitney Houston. If I feel this bad and didn't even know her; I can only imagine how her mother and her family are grieving. Never before in my lifetime have I had an entertainer's death hit me as hard as her's. I pray that her soul finds rest and God comforts her family. I was really proud of the way her home going was celebrated. Tyler Perry and Kim Burrell blew me away! It really doesn't matter how she died; the important thing for us to remember is what she gave to the world. She is gone now, let her rest in peace, and thank you Whitney.

The only thing I would say to her daughter is be careful with family and money. Nothing separates a family like money. Believe me, I've been there and done that. It took me 68 years to learn that, but finally I did. I would suggest if she is going to give money to family members, give them just a little and wait for the feedback from them and she will get feedback. I only wished I had done it this way.

The unmitigated gall of John and Ken in Los Angeles to label Whitney a crack ho is unforgiveable. Apparently they never saw the Diane Sawyer interview with Whitney where she took unbridled anger at insinuating she used crack. In her defense she said, "I make too much money to do crack, crack is whack." And to call her a "ho" is beyond my comprehension. Did she ever give them any? If she had been a "ho" how would they know? Like she said, "she made too much money."

GREED

Glaxo Smith Kline

It never ceases to amaze me the amount of greed represented by mostly conservatives, the people who espouse morals and Christianity. I never would have thought there was such greed in the world, from corporate executives, to companies, to just plain folks. Take for example GSK (GlaxoSmithKline), agreed supposedly to a $3 Billion dollar settlement with the government for allegations the company advertised drugs not approved by the food and drug administration. It was alleged the company made over $18 Billion Dollars. So what is eighteen take away three? That still leaves them with a profit of $15 Billion. I'd gladly pay the 3 Billion dollars and laugh all the way to the bank. The only deterrent would be to take away all profits made on the products, and a fine. This way, the company does not profit at all.

Barclays

Who could have thought or believed the toppling of two executives in the midst of an expanding rate rigging scandal. I could go on and on with this list, but why bother? Then there are those who represent to me the lowest form of humanity. They are the ones who embezzle from the estates and trusts of the elderly and often incapacitated individuals, and charge exorbitant fees. I read recently where a Controller in the office is linked by probate records to wire transfers totaling 17.3 Million dollars from 35 individual accounts. How do you give one person authorization to transfer anything over $1,000 without a second signature or authorization when you are in a position of trust; especially with other people money? This is hard for me, a common lay person to comprehend; I wouldn't trust mama in this instance.

Major Divorces

You can see this anytime a major celeb, sport superstar or anyone having lots of money. I can't for the life of me understand why there is so much bickering over money. If each individual involved in the divorce has millions of dollars, why should you need to have as much as the other individual? It is not a necessity that you live the same glamorous lifestyle as you did when you were married; you didn't before you married the individual. At some point, you loved this person and had a close relationship with them. You had intimate relations with them, which may or may not have produced a child or children. You were so close you could have taken a pill and it would've worked the other partner also. Do you comprehend what I mean? All of a sudden, you can't stand your once great love. Why not chalk it up to a mistake, move on with your life and remain friends for the benefit of a child or children? You both end up paying lawyers copious amounts of money. For what? This is something you should've been able to work out yourselves.

My mother used a phrase all the time that said, "Before you get married you can eat each other up. Once you are married, you'll wish you had."

Bernie Madoff

Remember him?

This is just a few examples of greed. There is no need to name everyone. You get my drift.

ROBO-CALLS & JUNK MAIL

These are some of the most annoying calls you can receive. It really pisses me off to the highest degree of pissitivity to be talking on the phone and get a beep that there is another incoming call. You hurriedly end your call to pick up this call, and there is a recording that says, "Don't hang up." This is followed by a sales pitch. What is even more annoying is when you are called at 8 a.m., showing no regard for you. I have to do something! I am going to call the phone company and see what the cost is to have incoming calls show the phone number and person's calling displayed on your television. My son and his wife have that availability on their television.

We get so much junk mailings until I sit right next to the paper bin and toss all junk mail directly into that bin without even opening. So if you are one of the one's sending us junk mail, you're wasting your postage. Stop!

Attorney General Eric Holder

Excuse me, but I think all the hoopla and "who shot John," combined with the innuendo and accusations is just a smokescreen or diversion until hopefully they can find something incriminating to try and pin on him. It is a shame and disgrace politics has become so sordid. They want to make a mockery out of him because he has been getting in their asses about certain issues that just aren't copastatic or right, such as the Voting Rights Act for one. If half the amount of time, energy or the money was spent on the economy, maybe, just maybe they could get something done.

VOTING RIGHTS ACT

Now Republicans have figured out a way to disqualify poor voters and people of color, and place them in the position where their vote doesn't count. There are some people today who are just as prejudiced and racist as they were in the 1950's and 60's, but they won't admit it. They are afraid to admit it even to themselves, so they continue to deny they are racist or prejudiced to themselves. They can try to justify their actions all they want to, but we know what the real reason is. It is as if they want to return to the Jim Crow era, but we are NOT going back. I don't think my mom ever got the chance to vote, because she couldn't read nor write.

I remember asking her at one time who should we vote for, and her explanation was short and simple. She said to me, "It really doesn't matter too much, but we seem to do a little better if there's a Democrat as President."

I can guarantee you one thing, if the poor Whites vote for a Republican, they think they're having a hard time now, they will live to regret it. They haven't seen a hard time yet. President Obama may not seem to some that he is the right choice, but if you are looking for the lesser of two evils, President Obama wins hands down. Why do you think a man worth over $250 Million dollars can identify with you or care? He is only interested in the clout the President of the United States carries and what benefits he can offer his Super Pac friends.

If I sound pissed off, irritated, disillusioned or angry, it is because I am all of the above. I am fed up with Congress and all the infighting that goes on. No one is truly interested in what benefits America and what Americans want. If they were, they would work together as a unit to solve issues affecting all Americans.

When was the last time something positive was proposed to increase or encourage more voter participation by the masses?

God bless America!

www.ingramcontent.com/pod-product-compliance
Lightning Source LLC
Chambersburg PA
CBHW030356290526
45785CB00004B/1772